# The
essentials of major
gift fundraising

*by Neil Sloggie*

Published by
The White Lion Press Limited
Kermarquer
56310 Melrand
France

© 2005 Neil Sloggie/The White Lion Press Limited
ISBN 0-9518971-7-9

First printed 2005

Models: Gillian Egan and Ernst Goetschi

Photography by Adrian Taylor

Design and print production by em associates

Printed and bound in the United Kingdom by
The Baskerville Press, Salisbury

# Tiny

White Lion
Press

essentials of major
gift fundraising

# Contents

1   Stages of major donor fundraising

5   Finding the potential major donors

11   What should we ask the donor for?

17   Meeting the donor

25   Asking for money

30   The critical obstacle

33   Touching on philanthropic gifts
     from corporations

37   A word about grant giving
     foundations

43   Spending the money

45   A word on capital campaigns

51   Involving the CEO

# The author

Neil Sloggie's fundraising career spans 15 years. During this time Neil has worked with a wide range of organisations in Europe, Asia, North and South America, and in Australia and New Zealand, and he has made use of all fundraising techniques. Posts Neil has held have included Asia Pacific Region Fundraising Manager for Greenpeace International, Fundraising Manager for a London-based cancer charity, and senior consultant in a UK-based fundraising consultancy.

Neil is now a fundraising consultant based in Australia. He works in Australia and internationally with a range of clients. He is author of the highly acclaimed *Tiny Essentials of Fundraising*.

Neil Sloggie
Telephone: +61 (0)41 1304 7905
Fax: +61 (0)7 3105 7313
Email: neil@fundraisingsolutions.com.au
www.fundraisingsolutions.com.au

# Preface

Few fundraising specialisms hold more promise than the personal individual development of potential major donors. Equally, few areas of fundraising have hitherto been so neglected.

But that's all in the past. Once again, internationally respected fundraising consultant Neil Sloggie explains and illustrates the tiny essentials of a major area of fundraising. This time through the instructive experiences of Daniel and the Clean Green Fund for the Environment, Neil shares his knowledge with other fundraisers. He describes all the stages of a major gift programme from the initial research – and how to go about it – through to donor cultivation and solicitation, even to the pitfalls you could face when you achieve success.

This book can be read inside an hour, leaving you free to put its lessons into practice immediately you put it down.

# About the 'Tiny Essentials' series

The book you hold in your hands is part of a series of little books with a big mission. They each focus on what really matters in one key area of voluntary sector management. Each book's purpose is to provide the essentials of its subject in a readable, easily digestible form, so people who otherwise wouldn't dream of reading a business book can effortlessly and enjoyably get access to what they really need to know.

Books in the 'Tiny Essentials' series are delightfully free of padding, waffle and overblown theories. Extraneous material has been reduced to a minimum. Each book so lives up to its title that there's just no room for anything other than the essence of what really matters in the subject area, and how to order your priorities.

This 'Tiny' focuses on what every fundraiser, CEO and board member needs to know about establishing and developing a major donor fundraising strategy. Other books published or planned in the 'Tiny' series include:

*Tiny Essentials of Fundraising*, by Neil Sloggie

*Tiny Essentials of Writing for Fundraising*, by George Smith

*Tiny Essentials of an Effective Volunteer Board*, by Ken Burnett (to be published in 2005).

*Tiny Essentials of Raising Money from Trusts and Foundations*, by Jo Habib (to be published in 2006).

*Tiny Essentials of Fundraising Strategy*, by Maggie Taylor (to be published in 2006).

*Tiny Essentials of Monthly Committed Giving*, by Harvey McKinnon (to be published in 2006).

*Tiny Essentials of Legacy Fundraising*, by George Smith (to be published in 2006).

All can be ordered on www.whitelionpress.com

# Stages of major donor fundraising

It all started one Wednesday afternoon about two years ago. That being the day of the month when the automatic payment debit went through, I was in a fairly happy mood. It does the soul of all fundraising managers good to send a request to a bank to debit the accounts of several thousand regular donors who give by automatic payments – and watch money roll towards a cause that really needs it.

This day was particularly heartwarming. The previous month's very successful upgrade programme had persuaded about a third of our autopayment donors to increase their monthly gift, meaning a substantial increase in the cash available for Clean Green Fund's work. I watched as the team set the debit running. It went without a hitch and I looked forward to a leisurely afternoon.

I was surprised when a gloomy looking Ted, the scarily clever fundraising assistant, came into my room to tell me we had a problem. 'Problems are just opportunities Ted', said I with, on this occasion, a curious presentiment.

Ted had been going through the new monthly payments of the day and had noticed one from Mr John Sheridan, for £50. Well, I thought this was rather good. A monthly donation of £50 was above average for our humble organisation at that time. Ted, however, is someone who tends to put his finger on issues that need attention, so I waited expectantly to hear the flaw. Flaw indeed there was. Mr Sheridan turned out, on investigation, to be *the* Mr Sheridan, of Sheridan's Bank, a leading city institution in which our donor had an interest reputed to total more than £500 million.

This put a £50 donation in a rather different light. After some quick calculations on wage differentials, the highly numerate Ted had worked out that if we were asking those on average wages for a £50 donation we should be asking the likes of Mr Sheridan of Sheridan's Bank for more like £25,000.

I thought this to be fair reckoning, but suggested to my colleague that one just didn't see direct mail letters or emails floating around asking for donations of £25,000 per month. Our agency had baulked at sending out requests for an extra monthly £20 from our regular donors.

That seemed to end the discussion.

For the remainder of the day I pondered on how mean the very rich can be until I had my thoughts challenged at that evening's fundraising institute reception. It was my first visit to that learned group in some considerable time.

When I arrived I was pleased to see immediately the very pleasant and extremely successful Jacqui from the Blind Society. It was always something of an honour to meet this rather famous fundraising personality. I usually came away somewhat humbled and a little wiser; on this occasion both sensations were propelled to their extremes. I had mentioned confidentially (as we fundraisers sometimes do) the meanness of certain wealthy donors. In reply, she had informed me that our Mr Sheridan of the £50 donation had, only two months earlier, given a donation of £1 million to the Blind Society.

I reeled slightly in surprise, but managed to garble out a few words of response along the lines of, 'that would have increased the average gift to the appeal a bit Jacqui!' Jacqui delivered her usual sympathetic and understanding smile, while telling me that Mr Sheridan had not responded to a direct mail request, but to a personal ask, a solicitation face to face indeed, carried out by her and the chair of her board.

Now, dear reader, the thought of getting face to

face with a donor was, I confess, something that had not kept me awake at night in anticipation. I had rather assumed that most successful fundraising could be achieved without having much personal contact with the donor. Jacqui enlightened me with some further examples, which proved that the high level person-to-person approach was indeed successful and was an area in which her organisation appeared to have an ongoing programme of some intensity.

I mulled the whole thing over the next day with Ted. We concluded that we really did not have the measure of this phenomenon. Fortunately Jacqui had given me a few tips on how to take the matter forward, so that I didn't need to look completely out of my depth in front of my theoretical subordinate. Jacqui had said, 'Think about it in stages Daniel,

## 'One is the research, finding the potential major donors.

## Two is developing your case for support.

## Three is the initial meeting.

## Four is the actual solicitation.

## Five is the follow-up and beginning of the process of resolicitation.'

# Finding the potential major donors

I brewed Ted a tasty herbal tea as he considered the stages. When the beverage was supplied, I went on to relay the more detailed information Jacqui had divulged regarding stage one – carrying out research to find the potential major donors. She had said that if we wanted to start a major donor programme then we should research our existing donors first.

According to Jacqui, loads of organisations have developed huge lists of small donors through extensive direct marketing programmes. However, some never really research their donorbases properly to find out if there are any exceedingly rich people there who, given the opportunity, might give a very large gift. Jacqui explained that, in some countries, there are companies offering this service. They generally have their own list of very rich people, which they will run against a charity's fundraising database to find out if any of their rich people are hiding amongst the charity's donors.

She also said that we could do our own research by comparing the lists of the rich published in the press and other directories of company directors, or other influential people with our database. And she advised us that we should keep an eye on the press every day for stories of people suddenly becoming wealthy and then check our database in case they were donors of ours.

I suggested to Ted that we should do this research and if we found any more hidden wealthy people we could, well, we could maybe then go and ask Jacqui what to do next.

Ted then told me about one of the workshops that he had been to at a fundraising conference. It had been given by a major gift specialist fundraiser who seemed to know a thing or two. This person, a gentleman with a large booming voice, had said, 'CIA'. Just as I was wondering what we were getting into here, Ted explained that these letters stand for contact, interest and ability. 'These', the gentleman of major gifts had explained, 'are critical elements in the identification of a potential major donor.'

First he had suggested that fundraisers should build a list of people who might have the *ability* to make a major donation to their cause. This word ability is, in fact, just major gift code for people who are very rich. 'Once you have this so-called ability list', the specialist had said to Ted and his colleagues, 'you can research the people included to see if they have any *interest* in your cause.'

However, the specialist had emphasised that individuals who have heaps of money aren't usually too keen to have fundraisers just turn up at lunch-time on a Sunday with a hungry look, to discuss how much money they are going to give away that day. In fact it can be a little tricky to get in to talk to them at all, which is where *contact* comes in. If we can find someone who knows the rich, interested person, who can introduce us and help us present our cause to them, we're on to a very good thing.

Ted, after recalling all this from his participation at the workshop, went on to sum up for me his conclusions about it all. 'First we have to make a list of rich people. Second, we have to narrow that list down by finding out if anyone on it has shown an interest in our cause. Then we present the final list to our board members, contacts, volunteers and staff to establish if any of them knows someone on the list.'

This all sounded very good indeed. We tried to apply the thinking to our situation. Back then, we had 20,000 donors on our database. We thought that all of them must have interest (because they'd already been interested enough to donate). They also already had some degree of contact (we phoned or wrote to them regularly, so we could get in touch without a problem). All we needed to do was to find out who had ability (i.e. who had loads of money).

Suddenly Jacqui's advice to us became blindingly clear. We already had a large number of people with the contact and interest elements of CIA. Researching the database to find out if any of our donors were rich could possibly give us a ready list of people with all three CIA criteria. This would fit in very conveniently with the teachings of Ted's major gifts gentleman.

Ted took upon himself the task of researching the donors in our database. He got one of those companies with existing databases of the wealthy to help us and he did some of his own research with rich lists, directories and so on. This involved him sitting with a national newspaper's list of the 500 wealthiest in the nation and painstakingly plugging the names, one by one, into the database to see if they matched our donors.

One month later, Ted reported back. To our utter astonishment, from our list of 20,000, *no fewer than 50 extremely wealthy* people were identified. Here were top prospects, all of whom could afford to make very large donations. And we had been asking them all for regular gifts of between £10 and £50 per month. And that was exactly the level at which they were giving.

'It is time for action', I informed my colleague. 'We

will ensure that all of these 50 people will be given the opportunity to give to their maximum capacity. And', said I grandly, 'I am going to tell you just how we are going to do that, just as soon as I have had another meeting with the excellent and famously successful Jacqui of the Blind Society.'

Jacqui as it turned out was coming along to a little fundraisers' gathering that evening, organised by the local chapter of the fundraising institute in a private room at a local wine bar. I bowled along at the given hour. Alas, Jacqui's ear was grabbed almost exclusively by younger fundraisers for the entire evening and the best I could do was to get her agreement to meet me again at a future, but unspecified, date. However, by coincidence I got the advice I immediately needed from the formal presentation given to us at the meeting. The speaker that evening, called Nina, was talking about major gifts and she described exactly the stage we needed to move to with our programme.

... From our list of 20,000 no fewer than 50 extremely wealthy people were identified.

Nina also talked about major gift fundraising from either the contact, ability, or interest angle. She confirmed that you can usually assume your donors have contact and interest, so you just need to research their ability, just as Ted and I had been doing, in order to create an initial target list.

According to Nina, you can also approach major gift fundraising by *starting* with contact. This involves *contact networking*, which is simply chatting with as many people connected with your organisation as possible and asking them if they know any rich people and, particularly, if they can count rich people amongst their friends. Their memories can be jogged by showing them lists of the rich. If someone identifies her best friend amongst the lists of the rich, you have established two of the three golden words – contact and ability – and if the person has shown any interest in the past in the organisation's cause then he or she is worth adding to your target list.

I left the room just for a moment to gather up my thoughts. I concluded that stage one is the research, finding the potential major donors, so we had to,

**List donors with contact, ability (wealth) and interest.**

**Research our donorbase for these wealthy people.**

**Interview board members and all others connected with our organisation to see if they have any contact with wealthy people.**

# What should we ask the donor for?

Back at the fundraisers' meeting, Nina was entering stage two of her speech. 'Then you need a "case for support". Don't be alarmed', she went on to explain, 'this is jargon for just figuring out the things you need money for.

'Typically this can be an overall plan with a budget, or individual projects or items, which have different costs attached. Some fundraisers call this the shopping list, a selection of good stuff the organisation needs, with costs attached. There can be items for £10,000, or for £10 million, to be presented to donors according to how much you reckon they can readily afford to give.'

But, as fundraisers who have been around a while will know, this subject can be a little tricky for some organisations. Such a document will not exist for all charities. It is often up to us fundraisers, together with the programme director or CEO, maybe both, to figure out simple answers to the donor's likely question, 'If I give you £20,000 what will it be used for?' Or, 'if I were to give you £500,000 what would you use it for?'

'The secret to building a case for support', said the excellent Nina, 'is *to figure out exactly the output of the organisation and how much this output costs, so that you have something clear and measurable to offer donors.*

'This is comparatively easy for those of you working with charities that help people. You can just divide the overall organisational budget by the number of people you help and then you have a figure for what it costs to help one person. Or, you can look at individual projects and do the same thing. You can then multiply the figure to fit whatever you think the donor can afford.

'For example, an emergency telephone helpline type organisation might help 10,000 people a year, at a cost of £1,000,000. So it costs £100 to help each person. And if a donor can give you £100,000 you can say with hand on heart that he or she is providing emergency support to 1,000 people who are desperately in need. Donors feel good about this sort of thing because they can easily create a mental picture of what their gift will achieve.

'This approach can be broken into projects for bigger organisations – how many people it will help, how much it will cost – then you have a proposal for a donor based on how many people he or she can help with £50,000, or whatever.'

I thought about the output of our organisation, which exists to help save the environment. It was a bit less clear than specific numbers of people, but I did see that we could say we were working towards a tangible reduction in one environmental problem by one campaign we were running and that we would conserve one area of land with another project. Each of these could be costed.

*... The main issues for the donor are usually – how exactly is it going to help, and how much will it cost?*

Other organisations might have clear plans about projects they wish to undertake, with clear budgets attached. Again the main issues for the donor are usually: how exactly is it going to help, and how much will it cost?

Nina again mentioned creating a 'shopping list' of opportunities to give. For example: next year it is going to cost us £50,000 to do X, £150,000 to do Y, and £300,000 to do Z.

She said that the case statement can be designed as a formal brochure, but that it is sometimes better to have a group of projects arranged loose in a smart folder. This gives you the opportunity, if you have a lot of projects needing funds, to select those more likely to appeal to specific donors, or more likely to be at the level they can afford, for each individual you meet.

'By the way', Nina said, 'always try to build your case for support on the basis of the actual service or work you are doing, like the example of the emergency telephone helpline folks.'

Donors in her (and now my) experience prefer to help the actual cause than to buy you new shelving for the computer room, or to pay for a consultant to untangle the wires. They also prefer to give a donation as a result of you showing how it will help people in desperate need, or something directly related to your organisation's cause, rather than because it happens to be your organisation's fiftieth anniversary, or some other issue related more to the organisation than to the cause. I know it has been said before, but it always seems to need saying again: organisations are set up to help a cause, usually they are not a cause in themselves.

Nina gave some useful parting advice. She said, 'It has always seemed awfully sensible to me, to figure out what you actually need prior to going to visit a donor. I've subsequently been very glad of it because some of these rich types can come very directly to the point and say "just tell me what you need" within about two minutes of you walking through their door. If you don't know the answer to this question you are in trouble. Other donors take a lot longer to get to this point and it can be handy to have "a shopping list" to whip out and discuss to bring a focus back to the meeting.'

So, I had what I wanted from this most instructive evening, but it didn't end there. Experienced fundraisers know that at these events half of what you learn is in the corridors outside the presentations. We had some drinks later and Nina, when I cornered her, delivered a couple of additional, rather important hints on the subject of case building that I'll try to relate here.

*... Organisations are set up to help a cause, usually they are not a cause in themselves.*

She said, 'It is important *that the shopping list includes items for support that your organisation already has planned.* For example, you can say that you need £50,000 to help 500 people next year, or £200,000 to help 2,000 people, or you have an issue you wish to work on that has a clear objective and will have an overall cost of £100,000. The fact that you were already going to work on these anyway with your forecast fundraising income from other areas is immaterial, because you can never rely on fundraising income 100 per cent. So you can't guarantee that it will happen, unless the donor pays for it. Other items on the shopping list could be "wish list" items, completely new items or areas needing funds, which everybody in the organisation has agreed are priorities.'

At the end of the evening I added a few more notes,

**We need funding propositions to discuss with donors.**

**These funding propositions make up what we call our 'case for support', or 'case statement'.**

**These can be clearly costed plans.**

**Or they can be costed measurements of output. It costs X to help one person, or, in the Clean Green Fund's case, it costs X to save this piece of land.**

**Funding propositions should usually be more about the great work of the organisation and less about the organisation itself.**

**We should try to concentrate the donor on our existing work, to ensure that it is funded before embarking on new work.**

# Meeting the donor

It had been a late night and the next morning I was at work a little later than scheduled. I decided to take Ted to the local café for a hearty breakfast, at about midday, to tell him all I had learned. The good man took it all on board. No sooner was our meal finished than he dashed off enthusiastically to get our new case statement together. I meanwhile decided to seek further advice from the highly knowledgeable Jacqui, so I walked straight to the headquarters of the Blind Society, which I discovered in a very grand building not far from the previous evening's wine bar.

Now I'd like to say that it is not in my nature usually to drop in unannounced on senior fundraisers in their offices. But I sometimes get the urge and I usually find that the most successful ones, bizarrely enough, aren't that busy. I also have found that often the most successful fundraisers are happy to share their knowledge. And I did indeed find Jacqui not particularly busy and happy to chat.

The essence of our conversation was this. I recounted to Jacqui how, through our research of existing donors, we had found 50 potential major donors, i.e. 50 people who were already giving to our organisation at a low level, who we now knew could afford to give lots more. I told her we would soon have an excellent case for support ready. Then I confessed that I would be very much obliged if she would kindly provide guidance as to what to do next.

Jacqui returned to her earlier advice again. 'Remember the stages Daniel', she said. 'Stage one is the research, finding the potential major donors. Stage two is developing your case for support. Stage three is the initial meeting. Stage four is the actual solicitation. Stage five is the follow-up and beginning of the process of resolicitation.

'Assuming you have discovered that an existing donor is rich and you have also found someone who knows the rich person well, I suggest that he or she should contact the donor to ask for a meeting. If you don't have someone who knows the donor, it is okay for the chairman or CEO to make contact. The person being contacted has already given money to your organisation so should not be surprised to hear from you.

'The purpose of the meeting, you can say in the letter, email, or phone call, is to thank them for their ongoing support and to update them on current developments. You can arrange to meet at the donor's home or office, or your office – whichever suits the donor. Either the person who knows the donor, or the chairman or CEO will do as the letter-writer. The letter-writer should ideally be at the meeting. And you should be there also Daniel, to keep the meeting focused.

'But', Jacqui continued, 'it is very important that you give the donor ample opportunity to talk throughout the entire meeting. He, or she, must feel able to comment or ask questions at any time.'

Once Jacqui started, she didn't seem to pause for breath. 'At the first meeting', she said, 'the first third of the meeting should be a general update. At this point, if you can, it's good to inspire the donor about achievements and the good work you are doing. The second third should be talking specifically about areas where support is needed. The last third can be used to answer the donor's questions and to enter into discussion regarding his or her donation, if that is appropriate.'

To be totally honest, all this didn't mean too much to Ted and me when we got our heads together the following morning, but we decided to make the best of what we had and just get on with the programme, as suggested by Jacqui. We suspected that in time and with the benefit of experience we would add substance to her advice.

I wrote individual letters from our chairman to the top 10 on our list of rich people that we had found on our donorbase. Then I trotted over to his office, got the necessary signature and sent it off to our big targets. The letter was pretty straightforward, just as we had been advised earlier, asking to see them to say thank you and to update them on our work. I'd taken the precaution of asking the chairman if he knew any of the people he was writing to, which was just as well, because he did know someone on the list and that person received a more personal letter.

The first person to respond basically told us to get lost, which was not too motivating. But the next said that yes, she would like to meet and could come to visit us the following week. I called her and the chairman to make the appointment and all was set for the following Wednesday. The CEO pulled rank and invited himself also to meet the rich visitor, which was fine but might possibly, as Jacqui had warned me, make the meeting more difficult to manage. This alarmed me a little because I was aware that Jacqui knew what she was talking about.

Our big day arrived. We had decided that our rich guest would be shown around our offices by the chairman, then brought to the CEO's office for coffee and to be given the chance to ask questions. At that point we would present her with our case statement, which showed what we were doing and explained, under some different gift amounts, what we needed for future work.

What actually happened was that the chairman and CEO were falling over each other to tell our prospect every detail about how our organisation worked, right down to the effect of weather on the staff's morale – always a major topic of conversation, I'm sad to admit. Our too-polite donor was given no opportunity for questions and the case statement wasn't even presented.

At the end of the meeting, I managed to guide the dear donor from the room to take her, on her own, to her car. On the way to the front door, she was able to ask me some questions. I answered as fully as I could, we discussed our most urgent needs in the car park and I handed her the case statement, which she said she'd consider. To my utter astonishment she had a quick look before ordering her driver into action and said she'd 'do something for us', whatever that meant. With greater excitement than attended the biggest mail campaign in history, I watched the letterbox over the following days and was rewarded with one of our biggest ever gifts, £50,000, a few days later.

The CEO was even more astounded than I was and wanted to know what the donor wished for in return. I looked at her letter, which demanded nothing. He couldn't believe it. Up until then he had been busy cultivating middle-management corporate donor types who had a budget of anything between £1 and £20,000 to give to charities, for which they were demanding little short of the right arm of every one of the charity's employees in recompense. In addition they insisted on years of advance guaranteed brand-building to shore up their companies' dubious reputations (which universally were in serious need of attention of the most fundamental nature).

Ted pointed out in his own incisive way that this major donor fundraising seemed easier and had a better return than anything we'd done in the past. And it was more fun said he, but then he had not been at the meeting with the CEO and chairman.

Over the weekend, I remembered Jacqui's description of the ideal meeting in three parts and her five points of good advice. Unfortunately my colleagues had not understood these in the briefing I'd given. We had discussed the three-part meeting:

- The first third of the meeting should be an inspirational general update.
- The second third should be talking specifically about areas where support is needed.
- The last third can be used to answer the donor's questions and to enter into discussion regarding his or her donation, if appropriate.

But they had ignored the three phases and, in fact, the meeting had progressed no further than the first part. There had been no opportunity to get onto Jacqui's next piece of advice regarding discussing donations, my colleagues had not listened to the donor and they had talked too much. If the donor had wanted to say 'I've got a million pounds for you', she wouldn't even have been heard. The only way I could use any of Jacqui's advice and refer to what we actually needed had been to shut my colleagues in the office and talk to the donor on the stairs and in the car park. More training of all involved was needed.

With this particular donor, over time, we did have further meetings. Because she had been so generous at that first, almost disastrous, meeting, subsequent get-togethers were very easy; we just had to show her how well her money was being spent. Once she got more involved we were able to solicit further larger gifts, armed with our greater understanding of how to conduct donor meetings.

However other donors were completely different. We realised that we had to deal with each potential major donor individually and to respond carefully to how each reacted. One donor was very interested in learning more about our cause and we arranged a follow-up meeting to give him further information, before he then decided to give. Another donor asked for a formal proposal with more detail than was included on our shopping list. And one donor was extremely enthusiastic, but never seemed to get to the point of committing to a donation.

We have learnt that as long as we can get the conversation around, either in the first or the second meeting, to what we actually need, or to our case statement or shopping list, the donor can usually be steered to a donation without requiring a direct request. We have also created a golden rule of our own: *that we must never leave any donor meeting without some follow-up planned*. Sometimes the meeting deals mainly with general issues, with no conclusion as to whether the donor will give, because we feel that the donor is not sufficiently warm to move to a clear ask. In cases like this we try to think of some reason for a further meeting, to show a particular part of our work, or to discuss further how the donor could help in future.

We discovered that very rich people often know each other. So a great conversation to have with one rich person is how he or she can help get a large donation from another rich person. Don't assume that such a request will be an imposition. Often, your rich prospect will agree gladly to help secure a gift from his or her friend. Sometimes from several friends.

The discussion can happen at any donor meeting, even before rich person one has agreed to donate. But if such donors are to become involved and give specific help in approaching another rich person, it can be strongly hinted that they will look bad if they do not give first!

The notes in my little book continued to grow,

### We must use the three-stage plan as a guide for our donor meetings.

### We must never leave any donor meeting without some follow-up planned.

### Major donors are sometimes the best contact available to other major donors.

# Asking for money

In our first meeting with a donor there had been that rather rushed talk about our range of opportunities on the way to the car. It had seemed to do the trick with that person, but I knew that in future we would need to be more precise and to get more directly to the point of asking the donor for money. I decided to hunt out Ted's earlier expert, the man who had spoken so knowledgeably at the conference of some time ago, to hear his view on the matter. It turned out that he is a fundraising consultant called Andrew and I was very pleased to pay for half a day of his time to come and give us a bit of a talking to on the subject.

He arrived at our office a few days later and I had arranged for Ted and our very busy CEO to join us for the talk. Andrew started by restating Jacqui's original stages:

- One is the research, finding the potential major donors.
- Two is developing your case for support.
- Three is the initial meeting.
- Four is the actual solicitation.
- Five is the follow-up and beginning of the process for resolicitation.

He then spent a little time going through the first three stages, which was pretty helpful really, because it confirmed much of what we had already learned. Then it was time for stage four.

'You have already found that stage four is not always needed', he said, 'and that the gift can come after just stage three. Often, once the needs of the organisation are revealed in a clear way in stage three, the donor will volunteer a gift of one of the items on your case statement. In fact you can guide the donor towards specific items or specific levels. You may have separate projects or shopping list items that require funds ranging from £20,000 to £500,000. If you know that the donor can afford gifts of over £100,000 – for instance because he or she has given such gifts to other organisations – you may wish to leave off all items needing funds of less than £100,000.

'But', said our wise consultant, 'there are some people who will need to be asked in a more clear way. You have already told me about the super-rich donor who is very enthusiastic but never seems to get to the point of committing. This person probably needs help to get him to a point to make a decision. Asking for money is simply a question of focusing the donor further on the needs, then giving him or her a very polite opportunity to commit.'

*In fact you can guide the donor towards specific items or specific needs.*

Ted was taking in every word and I was scribbling serious notes.

Andrew continued, 'My approach is to select the specific costed need of the organisation in which the donor has shown most interest, describe it – including the money needed to carry the project out – then pause. This in itself should elicit a response, however, if it doesn't you might like to use the wording: *would this be a good time to ask if you might consider contributing this amount to this area*? Although you are putting the donor on the spot to an extent, it is important to leave him or her ultimately some let out clause. In the example I just gave you, I asked if *this was a good time to ask*? Although this is a very direct question, it still gives the donor the opportunity to turn you down while leaving the door open for a future request.

'If you are not sure of a specific area the donor is particularly interested in, or if you are not completely clear what level he or she can afford, you could discuss a range of options, presenting the donor with a paper that lists project headings and amounts. You can then ask the donor, is there an area of our work on this table that you might be able to help us with?'

Ted, our CEO and I looked at each other. I think we were all worrying about being pushed into stage four and having to say these scary words. But Andrew went on to reassure us that when you've done it once, it is very easy to do again – the first time is the hardest. He also advised that the meeting should be held in as good a humour as possible, to smile a lot and to try consistently to put the donor at ease.

Andrew then went on to talk about *the importance of getting the right asker.* 'The CEO is fine, but if a potential major donor could be asked by another donor, who is a peer of his or hers, it could be more successful. Also if the ask is made by someone the donor particularly respects, or owes a favour to, this could add to the weight of the ask.

'But', he added, 'it is not always possible to find such an individual outside the organisation and there can come a time when you must move ahead with what you have. If the CEO or chair of the board can be trained in this work', he looked a little suspiciously at our CEO, 'then they can be appropriate askers.

'The last golden rule of the major donor meetings is the most important', said the very experienced Andrew. '*You must listen always to the donor.*' I felt the CEO looked a little uncomfortable at this, as if it had been directed to him. Andrew ploughed on, 'Some people will be a little nervous with donors, this can result in them talking too much and not listening. Donors may have questions, or be indicating that they are interested in another subject, or wish to bring the meeting to a close, or actually want to discuss a possible donation. You must', he said staring worryingly at the CEO as if he knew something he didn't, '*always listen to the donor* throughout these meetings.'

Well, there was a little awkward silence after the learned one departed, until the CEO said, 'That chap seems to know a thing or two, seemed to put his finger on the key issues didn't he?' This broke the ice and we were able to have a frank and constructive discussion about how we could develop our technique with donors in future.

My golden rule book was added to that night with the gems,

**Find the most appropriate asker.**

**Plan the ask amount and the subject.**

**Script the exact words of the ask using Andrew's wording as a guide.**

**Listen to the donor.**

# The critical obstacle

Early the following week Ted popped his head round the door to disclose the excellent news that three of our other potential major donors had agreed to meetings. I, however, was up to my ears approving the designs for our new line in greetings cards. Following that, I had to finalise arrangements for a very time-consuming special event that was at a crucial stage of preparation. I asked if our major donors could be put off for a week or so, then I might be able to get on top of things on the home front.

Ted raised his eyebrows in a manner that I knew spelled trouble, but he merely asked for a reminder as to the income produced annually from our greetings cards sales. 'Ted, £120,000 last year', said I, quick as a flash, having just been briefed by the design agency on this very subject. Ted mildly continued, 'And once design, print, production, delivery, publicity, staff and unsold stock costs are taken into account?'

*Major donor prospects... often have the ability to give substantial sums, for very little effort.*

I shimmied around in my response to this a bit, wondering, frankly, who would really want to go to that level of detail into such an obviously successful programme. Ted, however, was already on my computer and was able, without my help, to locate the required figure on a spreadsheet amongst some previously unvisited depths. He quietly answered my question as to why the very small figure was coloured red and in brackets.

I'm never usually at my swiftest mentally on Monday mornings, but on this occasion I quickly grasped the implications of Ted's thought train. In short, my clever colleague was shunting my attention from the highly engaging but low net income sidings of fundraising, back to the less immediately demanding but much higher netting main tracks of major gift fundraising.

This experience reminded me about one of the things Nina had said to me that night in the wine bar that I forgot to mention to you earlier dear reader. She said, '*Major gift fundraising is potentially an extremely high net income source to the organisation, but your attention is always demanded by lower netting programmes.*'

Fundraisers frequently learn from bitter experience that this is absolutely and terribly true. Major donor prospects do not demand attention like broken databases or looming special events, but often they do have the ability to give substantial sums, for very little effort. Someone working in major gifts needs to exert considerable discipline to ensure that major gifts fundraising remains near to the top of the priority pile.

The note underlined in my book is,

**Prioritise your work to ensure that there is enough time for major gifts fundraising.**

# Touching on philanthropic gifts from corporations

Well dear reader we had some fun and games during the following weeks with our approaches. The chairman was not able to come to the meetings, so the CEO and I had to do the honours and we worked out a pretty satisfactory double act. He did the general inspirational update, started talking specifics about what we needed and then opened the conversation to the donor.

If the donor showed interest the CEO got straight to the point by handing over the previously prepared case statement, with the shopping list figures included, for discussion. I peppered around in the background, just throwing in the odd reminder comment when the good CEO got too excited to listen, or got so carried away describing his favourite area that he forgot to move to the specifics and the numbers. On one occasion, the donor did not respond to the gentle tactics so the CEO was forced to move to stage four and make an actual request for money. On this occasion it was successful, which bolstered his confidence supremely.

We met some interesting people. There was the billionaire who turned up with his wife on the bus; then the shortly-to-be-bankrupt show-off in the luxury car; and a gentleman whom we rather cooled of, after those arms trade revelations in the Sunday newspapers.

By the way, I developed a theory, which I hold to this day, that often the more money people really have, the less showy they are and the less they want recognition for their gift.

One of the people on our top 50 list was the CEO of a hugely successful bank. This person had been lurking on our donor list for years, unknown to us, giving £100 per year. Meanwhile we had been roundly rejected by his establishment on several occasions when we had asked for a donation through the usual channels, i.e. a direct application to his corporate giving department. It also turned out that his brother was a personal friend of the chairman of the Clean Green Fund.

This Mr CEO agreed to meet my chairman and me at his office. After the usual update and questions he stated that he was extremely interested in our work and asked how he could help. My chairman gave him a copy of the case statement and directed his attention quickly to the high end of the shopping list at the back. Mr Seriously Rich Banker ran his finger over the figures, stopped at one of the largest and, to my amazement, said his bank could probably do that one. I asked what steps we should take and he replied that I should just apply through the usual channels, for this sum of £150,000, and he thought we'd have a good chance.

Now, considering we had been turned down twice for requests of just £5,000 I was a bit sceptical about this. However, we followed up immediately with an application through the usual channels – to the corporate giving department. My surprise was complete when I got a call from some previously anonymous person called the head of community relations, inviting me for coffee at the bank's head office. At that meeting she informed me that our application had 'struck a chord' with 'the committee' and 'it was likely that we would get the gift'. During the next five minutes, as I was goggling like an idiot, she made general pleasantries. She had just one request, the bank would like a plaque commemorating the gift somewhere and some information about how it would be used, for the internal staff magazine.

Well I left the meeting on air, as they say. And, having promised a plaque, with an unveiling ceremony, I went off to investigate where one bought plaques from. I picked one up for £50 and for a further £20 bought a rather silly set of curtains, complete with a little string to pull at the unveiling. Which seemed like a pretty fair investment for a gift of £150,000.

This fitted in with some other advice from my guru, the irreplaceable Jacqui from the Blind Society. She had told me that sometimes the biggest corporate donations are made to the pet interests and projects of the CEO.

Ultimately we found that, in addition to getting the CEO interested, if we could in some way match our organisation to the corporation's interests then we had the best chance for a large donation. Such an alignment of interests has helped keen corporate CEOs greatly in advocating our cause.

I wrote my key learning about philanthropic gifts from corporations in my book of golden rules,

**The corporate CEO is often the only one who can make decisions about unusually large donations.**

**Sometimes we can stimulate an irrational decision from a corporation by appealing in some way to the interests of the CEO. He or she is the key to the largest corporate gifts.**

# A word about grant giving foundations

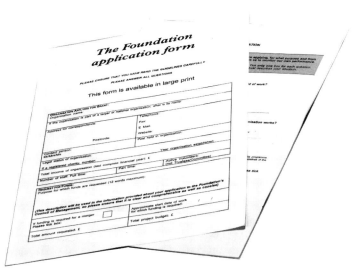

The Clean Green Fund had not previously considered grant giving foundations as a particularly serious source of money. This, of course, was because we were busy with those other very high maintenance areas of fundraising, from which it is hard to get away for even a moment. However, energised by our success at major gift fundraising from individuals and companies, we got started on the grant giving foundations and over time learned some golden rules for ourselves. Which I may say, I was able to impart with some pride to the mighty Jacqui of the Blind Society, who had but a fledgling programme in the area.

We discovered that grant giving foundations are institutions set up to give money away. Usually they have a capital amount, the earnings from which are distributed regularly to good causes on decision by a committee. Foundations we investigated ranged from tiny one-person affairs, to mighty international foundations with offices in many countries and support staff to screen applications to present to the committees.

We also discovered that in some countries larger corporations have set up company trusts to channel their charitable giving. These operate in much the same way as a foundation.

We went through the usual process of checking out foundations by using directories and the internet. We used as search criteria either the general aim of our organisation, or the specific projects we were working on and found foundations who accepted applications in this area. Through this process we built – and continue to build – a list of foundations that our research had indicated might be interested in receiving an application from us.

We discovered that grant giving foundations usually have information about how to make an application on their websites, or in the directories. And we found, after discussions with friends we made who work in foundations, that people who don't follow these guidelines are often amongst the first to have their applications rejected.

We consider the different organisations' guidelines very carefully, then put in a call to the foundation to discuss our application. Sometimes they don't want to talk. But we have found that more often they are happy to and can give very helpful information about how better to shape our applications. We also feel that once they start to talk about our applications, they can get enthusiastic about our work and this helps when the application reaches them.

*... We only found out about it when we didn't get the grant.*

After we send in an application, we now always call to ask if it has been received. We learned this golden rule when an application got lost in the post, we only found out about it when we didn't get the grant.

We also find out when the application will be considered by the committee and put in another call just prior to this date. This golden rule was learned when one committee member, after receiving his papers, raised a last minute question on a minor detail that the staff of the foundation were unable to answer. Because there was this unanswered question, the application was passed over in favour of one that they fully understood.

Our final golden rule is to look after the foundations extremely well after the grant is made. Usually they will need reports to some extent of what has been done with their money. We find out exactly what they need, make sure they get reports in plenty of time and call regularly to ensure there is nothing more that they would like. Thus, we become a favourite because we are easy to work with, so hopefully get more money in future.

As I said earlier, once you get to know your awfully rich donors they can introduce you to others. And so it is with foundations. At another meeting with that very wealthy woman I told you about earlier she introduced me to a friend, who didn't look rich in the least, but who turned out to be the chairperson of a grant giving foundation. She suggested we apply to the foundation and, well dear reader, once the chair of the foundation suggests you make an application, potentially, you're on a fast track to the land of largesse. In this case that is how it turned out. We secured yet another very big gift.

My suggestion then is that it's rather a good idea to check if you, or any of your board or other contacts, know the trustees of the foundation you are applying to. A helpful word in a trustee's ear can, in some cases, assist your application.

Our process, which includes all our golden rules,
is,

**Research the foundations.**

**Establish if anyone, either
inside or outside the
organisation, has a contact
in a foundation.**

**Determine those that are
suitable for an application.**

**Carefully read application
procedures.**

**Call the foundation for
further information and to
discuss the application.**

**Submit the application.**

**Call the foundation to
check the application has
been received and find out
when the decision will
be made.**

**Call the foundation a few
days before the decision is to
be made to ensure any last
minute questions are
answered.**

**Take great care to follow up
with all required reports.**

# Spending the money

Then, in the most extraordinary way, our major gifts programme started to give us a very serious problem. We became victims of our own success. People started to fight about spending the extra money.

Now this might all sound a bit odd, but it is a feature of major gifts programmes that in my opinion needs a bit of careful handling.

Supposing you raise a regular £5 million a year from a range of different fundraising methods, the staff in your organisation will breeze along as usual, expecting the usual annual budget negotiations to produce the usual small percentage rise or fall depending on 'prevailing economic conditions', which is sometimes just code for how competent the fundraising manager is.

Now throw a single £1 million donation in there and everyone knows there's some big time extra cash to be doled out. If the donor has chosen an item from a list of agreed priorities that are extra to the central budget (a type of 'wish list' shopping list), then he or she has already taken the decision about how the gift will be spent (although donors are often influenced by the fundraising manager).

But if not, then the CEO has an excellent opportunity to allocate extra funds to the areas most needing them at budget time. As with all funding issues, though, this does actually require a decision from the CEO about where the extra money is to go. Not all CEOs are as completely clear and confident in this area as they might be. Which means it can all turn into a bit of an argument.

The note for my book to come out of this was,

**The CEO has to be ready to make firm decisions about where any surplus will be allocated.**

# A word on capital campaigns

Now this little history is not really about capital campaigns, it is more related to programme organisations like mine. Capital campaigns are usually a big drive for exceptional specified sums required within a predetermined time-scale. They are more usually associated with one-off needs. A new hospital, or an endowment fund would be examples. But, even for an organisation like the Clean Green Fund, capital campaigns can be a handy technique to consider.

The multi-talented Jacqui was never too far from my thoughts in those ground-breaking days.

I found that as long as I bought her the occasional beverage of some description, she was willing to spill accumulated wisdom from her seemingly endless knowledge.

One weekend we met at the annual fundraising conference. I asked if I could trouble her for some guidance on capital campaigns and she agreed to take a little time out to talk with me. During a morning break, we went together in search of a warming brew and not far from the hotel we found a purveyor of fine coffee.

It turned out that Jacqui's organisation had been involved recently with a capital campaign and she started lecturing me at her usual speed. I did just manage to keep up and jot down the main points. According to Jacqui, 'The capital campaign is an opportunity to go for one-off, larger than usual gifts from existing donors, plus attract a whole new set of large donors into the organisation. It could raise big money quickly for an immediate need and, if you handle it properly, could give you a big extra resource of additional donors.'

She went on to tell me that capital campaigns are often run as one-offs by charities with very specific requirements, for which they need heaps of extra cash. The usual routine, apparently, is to spend ages figuring out exactly what is needed and how much it will cost down to the last detail; then to prepare just one case statement for a specific amount that is needed by a specific time.

Jacqui continued, 'This case statement should have

an overall target, broken down into a table of gifts that are required to meet the goal, otherwise known as a "gift range table". You know the sort of thing – one gift at £5 million, two at £3 million, five at £1 million and so on, are required to reach the total of £30 million to provide the new medical research building for the university, or whatever.

*... Capital campaigns can be a handy technique to consider.*

'First priority is to get the top gifts. Usually before the fanfare of a campaign launch, there's a so-called quiet period. This doesn't mean you're not working hard, rather that you are doing your best to find the prospective donors who could give you the biggest gifts and to work with them to try to get as many of them secured prior to launch.

'You can find them by using the same techniques as I mentioned before – either from your existing donors, or through research and contact networking. Approaches can also be similar to before, using whatever techniques of persuasion available – either the cause, or having a very influential person to ask them and then to steer them to the highest gift on the list they could possibly afford.'

The point about starting with the top gifts is awfully important. Jacqui emphasised, 'There is no point in starting a more general phase of a public appeal launch until you have the top gifts in.

Without the largest gifts on your gift range table, the campaign will fail. Getting those top gifts in first is your insurance that when you go public with a big launch it will be successful; and the fundraiser will not look stupid. Often successful capital campaigns will not be launched publicly until the vast majority of the total is raised in this quiet way.'

Jacqui told me there are a lot of highly experienced people in this area and it's really a good idea to get advice. In fact, as with other types of campaign, there are companies that can help you from start to finish. I reckon if I go down the capital campaign route I'll be going out and asking them what they could do for me.

These capital campaign experts can show you all sorts of tricks and techniques – ways to set up the gift range tables, numbers of prospects you would need, and so on – to make you confident that you will secure gifts. They will have the details for your particular situation, in your particular part of the world. Some rough guidelines, in Jacqui's opinion, are that the lead gift in a campaign should contribute at least 10 per cent of the total and at least 50 per cent of the total should come from the top 10 gifts.

It turned out that Jacqui had hired a capital campaign specialist consultancy to help her to plan her capital campaign. These consultants prepared for her what is called a feasibility study. She said that different organisations offer different types of these studies, but that the one she had retained had helped her to:

- Finalise the case statement.
- Assess organisational readiness (basically identify any obstacles to the campaign's success and figure out what needs to be done to fix them).
- Plan a gift range table.
- Assess likely levels of support for the gift range table through donor interviews and contact networking.
- Prepare a plan and budget for the capital campaign.

Very many people who are approached for large gifts to a capital campaign are quite new to the organisation; frequently they are not long-term donors already. I learned, therefore, that in this particular area of fundraising it's extremely important to get the asker right, that is the person who is asking for the gift on your behalf.

*Without the largest gifts on your gift range table the campaign will fail.*

As Andrew had already told us, it's important that potential major donors are asked by someone they respect. Usually this is someone whom they consider to be at least their peer, perhaps someone they owe a favour to, or someone who, for some reason, they find hard to refuse. With new donors you don't have your organisation's own credibility to rely on, because they have not been involved with giving any low amounts already like the folks I was talking about earlier.

My notes on capital campaigns are,

**The feasibility study conducted prior to launching a capital campaign will usually include: case statement, gift range table, organisational readiness, assessment of likely levels of support, and a campaign plan with budget.**

**First priority is to get the top gifts. Without these the campaign will fail.**

**Often capital campaigns will not be launched until lead gifts are secured.**

**Expert advice is widely available.**

**Where possible, potential donors should be asked by someone who has influence over them.**

# Involving the CEO

Jacqui and I zoomed back to the conference, partly because of the coffee but mainly because there was actually a speaker who had a real track record of success talking and we were keen to hear what he had to say.

That day was the last of the conference. In the evening there was a bit of a party, which I wandered along to. Jacqui was there and Nina. My dear colleague Ted came swinging in halfway through with a drink in each hand. The folks from our direct marketing agency, who I'd been neglecting for a while, wandered across for a bit of a friendly chat. And finally, our biggest convert to fundraising, our new leader in the major gifts area, Mr Enthusiastic himself, our CEO, was with us. He was leading the way in the general revelry. It was good to have him at last involved in fundraising and part of the team.

I thought about this a bit more later and realised that he hadn't been much involved in all our other fundraising. This is one area that really needs the CEO – and, in our case, needed significant amounts of his time. It wasn't an area in which he was personally experienced, but he was prepared to learn. What gave him the biggest buzz, and all the confidence, was actually succeeding.

I've since found that securing the CEO's time for this sort of work isn't always easy. CEOs are busy people. And if they're not experienced in the work, they can be a little scared by it and can find themselves avoiding it. But,

**Just one big success can change a reluctant CEO into an enthusiastic advocate. Success is the key.**

# A promise from The White Lion Press

Enjoy the best books on fundraising.

Books by The White Lion Press will repay your investment many times over – and you'll enjoy reading them too. But if your purchase is damaged in any way, or if you feel any of our products do not live up to your expectations simply return them to us and we will issue you with a full refund, including any reasonable associated costs. We'll ask you to tell us why, so we can put right anything that might be wrong, but we won't quibble. Unfortunately we can only offer this if you bought the book directly from us, but even if you didn't, please let us know your problem and we'll do all we can to ensure your supplier matches our commitment to you. After all, you are our ultimate customer.

This guarantee applies to any books or videos you may purchase from us. We further promise to handle your orders with speed, efficiency and impressive politeness.

You can order further copies of this book, or any of our other titles, from our secure website, www.whitelionpress.com. If you prefer, you can order by email, orders@whitelionpress.com; or fax, +33 (0)2 97 39 57 59; by post from Marie Burnett, The White Lion Press Limited, Kermarquer, 56310 Melrand, France, or by telephoning Marie on +33 (0)2 97 39 52 63. All books are also available from www.amazon.co.uk

# Tiny Essentials of Fundraising

by Neil Sloggie
Softback, 57 pp. ISBN 0-9518971-5-2

All you really need to know about fundraising, in one tiny book.

Join Kate, an inquisitive and ambitious new recruit to the fundraising profession, as she sets out to uncover what really matters in her chosen career by visiting and asking three seasoned practitioners. Like Kate you'll see as much to avoid as to emulate in the first two encounters but you'll be reassured and inspired as, in her final meeting, Kate discovers an organisation that has really thought through its fundraising strategy and approach, and shares with her – and you – the essential secrets of fundraising success.

'A simple and truthful reminder of what's at the heart of effective fundraising. How I wish someone had given me this book when I was starting out all those years ago!'
Jan Chisholm, Fundraising Manager, Greenpeace, Australia.

'I was given a copy of the 'Tiny' book in Australia and was so enamoured of the clear message it conveys that I ordered a special edition to give to more than 1,500 fundraisers and all 700 Blackbaud employees. Their reactions have been universally positive. *Tiny Essentials of Fundraising* is one of those books that make us truly envious of the author for executing such a brilliant piece of writing...'
Robert Sywolski, chief executive, Blackbaud Inc, USA.

'It's a smart idea, well-executed – how fabulous to have a bite-sized book that sums up what makes for successful fundraising in such an accessible way to both native and non-native English speakers.

'Great stuff. Thanks Neil for what must be the shortest, simplest and yet very salient contribution to the world's literature on fundraising.'
Julie Weston, UNHCR, Switzerland.

## Tiny Essentials of Writing for Fundraising

by George Smith
Softback, 65 pp. ISBN 0-9518971-6-0

'I suggest your heart would soar if – once
in a while – you received a letter written in
decent English which said unexpected
things in elegant ways, which moved you
and stirred your emotions, which angered
you or made you proud, a letter apparently
written by one individual to another
individual, For you never see these letters any
more…'

If you believe that words matter then this opinionated little book
is for you. For this 'Tiny' book will change forever the way you
and your organisation communicate.

'*Tiny Essentials of Writing for Fundraising* is a refreshing – and delightfully short – guide to the author's insights about the writer's craft. If
you're even thinking about writing fundraising letters you can't
afford not to buy this remarkable little book.'
Mal Warwick, chairman, Mal Warwick & Associates Inc, USA.

'I am a huge fan of George's blunt but refined writing, his clear and
individual voice, and his extraordinary ability to cut through the
crap – keep this wonderful little book next to your pen and pc.'
Lyndall Stein, CEO, Concern, UK.

'Smith is a self-confessed curmudgeon but nobody describes better
than he the power of words to advance your cause. The 11,149
words in this lovely book have been carefully selected and
assembled to help you write well enough to convince anyone of
anything.'
Ken Burnett, author, *Relationship Fundraising*; chairman, The Cascaid
Group, UK.

### Relationship Fundraising: A Donor-based Approach to the Business of Raising Money (second edition)

by Ken Burnett
Published by Jossey-Bass Inc in association with The White Lion Press Limited. Hardback, 384 pp. ISBN 0-7879-6089-6

Ken Burnett has completely revised and updated his classic book *Relationship Fundraising*. Filled with illustrative case examples, donor profiles, and more than 200 action points, this ground-breaking book shows fundraisers how to:

• Implement creative approaches to relationship-building fundraising.

• Avoid common fundraising errors and pitfalls.

• Apply the vital ingredients for fundraising success.

• Build good relationships with donors through marketing.

• Achieve a greater understanding of donors.

• Communicate effectively with donors – using direct mail, the press, television, the telephone, face-to-face contact, and more.

• Prepare for the challenges of twenty-first century fundraising.

'Not since Harold Seymour's classic, *Designs for Fund Raising*, has a book of this magnitude come along.

'Ken Burnett's updated and expanded work, *Relationship Fundraising*, just may be the book to which fundraising professionals turn for the next several decades.

'It is as brilliant as it is heartfelt, as simple as it is eloquent.'
Jerry Cianciolo, *The Compleat Professional's Library*, *Contributions Magazine*, USA.

'Ken Burnett's observations, insights and practical tips for building and sustaining relationships are superb. Highly readable, this book is a solid mix of sound theory and pragmatic application.'
Kay Sprinkel Grace, author, *Beyond Fund Raising*; co-author *High Impact Philanthropy*, USA.

'This is the book that sets the agenda for fundraising communications in the twenty-first century. Engaging, inspiring, and thought-provoking, *Relationship Fundraising* is based on the unique 25-year experience of one of the world's most respected fundraisers.'
Bernard Ross, director, The Management Centre, UK; co-author, *Breakthrough Thinking for Nonprofit Organizations.*

## Friends for Life: Relationship Fundraising in Practice

by Ken Burnett
Hardback, 599 pp. ISBN 0-9518971-2-8

Amid the widespread acclaim that greeted the 1992 publication of Ken Burnett's *Relationship Fundraising* was one persistent qualified comment. Essentially the question was 'relationship fundraising sounds very attractive, but will it help us raise more money?'

In this accessible and entertaining sequel, Ken Burnett describes how relationship fundraising is working in a wide variety of organisations in the USA, Canada and the United Kingdom. Their stories provide the answer: a loud and resounding 'yes!'

But the ideas and experiences described in this book will do much more than just help fundraisers raise more money. They will show them how to develop and maintain strong, healthy, mutually beneficial relationships with their donors; relationships that will enable them to make friends for life.

The sequel to *Relationship Fundraising* first appeared in 1996, to international acclaim.

'I'm an enthusiastic fan of Ken Burnett's approach to building friends for life. His new book builds on the practical, common-sense approach to donor development he is famous for advocating.

'Great examples, an easy read – I highly recommend *Friends for Life: Relationship Fundraising in Practice.*'
Dr Judith E Nichols, CFRE, author and consultant, USA.

'*Friends for Life* is a witty, readable tour of donor-think from both sides of the Atlantic and brings together a unique collection of experiences and anecdotes from many world-class fundraisers. *Relationship Fundraising* is already a classic throughout the world and this sequel is sure to have a similar impact.'
Jennie Thompson, consultant and co-founder of Craver, Mathews, Smith and Company, USA.

'The Botton Village case history is riveting. Its lessons have a relevance beyond fundraising. This is what direct marketing should always be, but so seldom is.'
Graeme McCorkell, author and consultant, UK.

## Asking Properly: The Art of Creative Fundraising

by George Smith
Hardback, 220 pp. ISBN 0-9518971-1-X

You will never read a book quite like this. George Smith tears open the conventional wisdom of fundraising creativity and so changes the rules for an entire trade. This book is irreverent, funny, savagely critical and genuinely inspiring, often on the same page.

*Asking Properly* is almost certainly the most authoritative book ever written about the creative aspects of fundraising. It is likely to remain a key text for years to come.

The author offers a profound analysis of donor motivation and is critical of the extent to which charities take their supporters for granted. But this book is no mere commentary on current practice – it offers a comprehensive checklist on how to optimise the creative presentation of the fundraising message. How to write, design, use direct mail, press advertising, broadcast media and the telephone, how to think in terms of fundraising products... the whole gallery of creativity and media is surveyed and assessed, with hundreds of examples of fundraising campaigns from around the world illustrating the need to 'ask properly'.

The book will prove invaluable to anyone involved in the

fundraising process. It is provocative, entertaining and, above all, highly instructive. Read it, apply its lessons and it must enable you to raise more money.

'This book will become a classic. It's not just inspirational and a great read, there's a practical benefit on every page. When you apply George Smith's secrets you can hardly fail to improve your fundraising.'
Harvey McKinnon, president, Harvey McKinnon & Associates, Canada.

'It's typically George Smith: wise, uncompromising, devastatingly critical of poor fundraising, brilliantly illustrative of what is good, full of ideas, funny, marvellously written – and exceptionally good value. In short, *Asking Properly* is one of those very few books you will keep for life.'
Pierre-Bernard Le Bas, head of fundraising, UNHCR, Switzerland.

## *Friends for Life* video series

A series of half hour videos from the Friends for Life sessions featuring Ken Burnett in Vancouver, Canada in July 1996. Filmed by Canada's Knowledge Network and produced jointly by Harvey McKinnon & Associates and The White Lion Press.

### Video One

• The challenge of relationship fundraising.

• How to introduce world-class donor service.

• Getting ahead of your competition.

### Video Two

• Botton Village: the classic case history of superb relationship fundraising.

• How you can profit from your donor's will.

• Four highly successful fundraising programmes.